Contents

What is a bat?

A bat is a flying mammal. Mammals feed their young on milk and most of them have hair or fur. Bats are the only mammals that can fly properly, although some other mammals can glide.

Is a bat a mammal?

Yes, a bat is a mammal.

Is a mouse a mammal?

Yes, a mouse is a mammal.

Like bats, mice feed their young on milk and are covered with a coat of hair. Mice belong to a group of mammals called rodents, which also includes squirrels and rats. Rodents' front teeth keep growing all through their lives. They keep them worn down by gnawing.

Butterflies have wings and can fly like bats can, but they are not mammals. Butterfly young – caterpillars – feed themselves. They eat the leaves on which they hatch. A butterfly is an insect. Like all insects, it has six legs.

Is a butterfly a mammal?

No, a butterfly is an insect.

Scary Creatures
BATS

Written by
Daniel Gilpin

Illustrated by
Bob Hersey

Created and designed by
David Salariya

Author:

Daniel Gilpin studied zoology at Bristol University before becoming a professional natural history author. This is his tenth book.

Artist:

Bob Hersey has worked in many mediums, including designing 3-dimensional models, artwork for advertising and illustrating children's books. He lives in Sevenoaks, Kent.

Additional artists:
Carolyn Scrace
David Stewart

Series creator:

David Salariya was born in Dundee, Scotland. In 1989 he established The Salariya Book Company. He has illustrated a wide range of books and has created many new series for publishers in the UK and overseas. He lives in Brighton with his wife, illustrator Shirley Willis, and their son.

Editor: Karen Barker Smith

Assistant Editor: Michael Ford

Picture research: Matt Packer

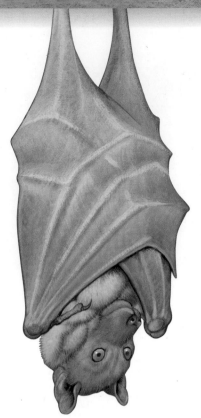

Published in Great Britain in 2004 by
Book House, an imprint of
The Salariya Book Company Ltd
25 Marlborough Place, Brighton BN1 1UB

Visit the Salariya Book Company at
www.salariya.com
www.book-house.co.uk

A catalogue record for this book is available from the British Library.

ISBN 1 904642 18 7

Printed in China.

Printed on paper from sustainable forests.

Photographic credits:

Bettman/CORBIS: 27
Getty Images: 24
Melvin Grey /NHPA: 13, 21
Daniel Heuclin/NHPA: 7, 8, 21, 23
Christoph Kappel/naturepl.com: 5
Hugh Maynard/naturepl.com: 26b
Mountain High Maps/©1993 Digital Wisdom Inc: 28-29
Dietmar Nill/naturepl.com: 15
Richard T. Nowitz/CORBIS: 26t
Tim Page/CORBIS: 7
©Merlin D Tuttle, bat conservation international: 18
Rod Planck/NHPA: 25
Adrian Warren/Last Refuge Ltd: 16

Every effort has been made to trace copyright holders. The Salariya Book Company apologises for any unintentional omissions and would be pleased, in such cases, to add an acknowledgement in future editions.

Pallidus bat in flight

Bats fall into two main types. The smaller type eats insects or meat. The larger type feeds on fruit or the nectar from flowers. The bat pictured above hunts flying insects such as moths.

Did you know?

There are more than 950 different species (types) of bat in the world. Britain has 16 species.

How big are bats?

Bats come in a variety of sizes. Most of them are small – not much bigger than a mouse with wings. Britain's biggest bat, the noctule, is just over 8 centimetres long. The smallest in Britain, the common pipistrelle, measures around 4 cm.

The world's smallest bat is Kitti's hog-nosed bat (above). They measure just 3.3 cm long and weigh just 2 grams. This type of bat is so tiny that it could sit on your finger.

Did you know?

Kitti's hog-nosed bat was not discovered until 1973. Not only is it the world's smallest bat, but is also the world's smallest mammal.

The biggest bats are those that eat fruit. They are known as fruit bats. Fruit bats live in hot countries where their food grows all year round. They feed by night and spend the day hanging from the branches of trees.

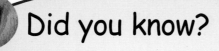

Spotted bat

The spotted bat from western North America is a medium-sized insect-eating species, with a wingspan of 35 cm. Its huge, pink ears are the largest of any North American bat. At 5 cm in length, they are almost as long as its body!

Indian flying fox

The largest fruit bats are known as flying foxes. Although they are not quite as big as a real fox, they are very large indeed. The world's biggest bat is the kalong, a type of flying fox from Indonesia. Its wings measure more than 1.5 m from one tip to the other. Another very large bat is the Indian flying fox (left).

Bats' wings are much longer than their bodies. This boy is holding a fruit bat (below), showing its relatively large wingspan.

Boy with a fruit bat, showing its wingspan

How do bats fly?

Bats fly in the same way as birds and insects – by flapping their wings. As a bat's wings flap downwards they push against the air underneath them, forcing the bat itself up. On the upstroke, the bat turns its wings at an angle so that they slice through the air.

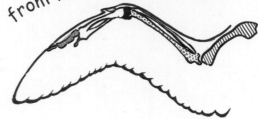

A bird's bones support muscles from which feathers grow.

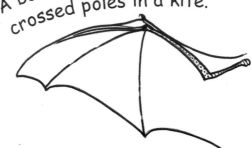

A bat's bones support skin like the crossed poles in a kite.

Comparison between a bird's wing and a bat's wing

X-Ray Vision

Hold the page opposite up to the light and see what's inside a Natterer's bat.

See what's inside

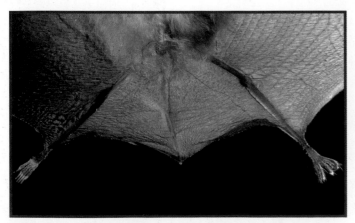

Skin stretched between the legs and tail of a bat

Bats' wings are made from thin membranes of skin stretched between the body, legs and long finger bones. In some bats, the wing membrane also stretches between the legs and tail (left). Most bats have four fingers built into the wing membrane itself. The fifth finger, or thumb, forms a claw which the bat uses to help it clamber around.

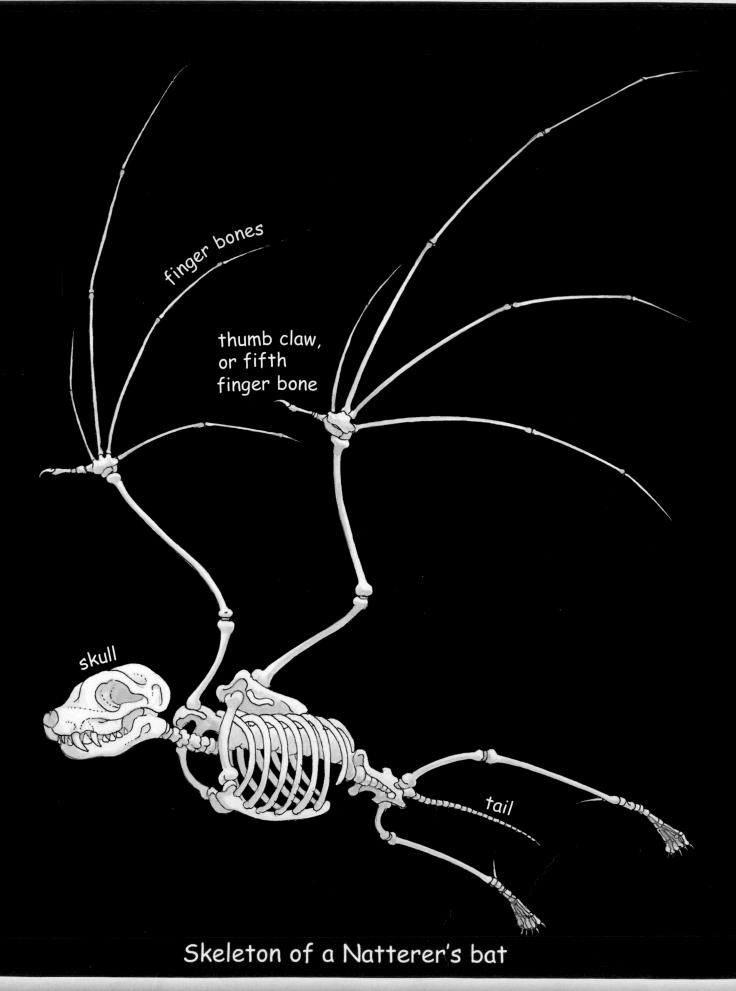

finger bones

thumb claw,
or fifth
finger bone

skull

tail

Skeleton of a Natterer's bat

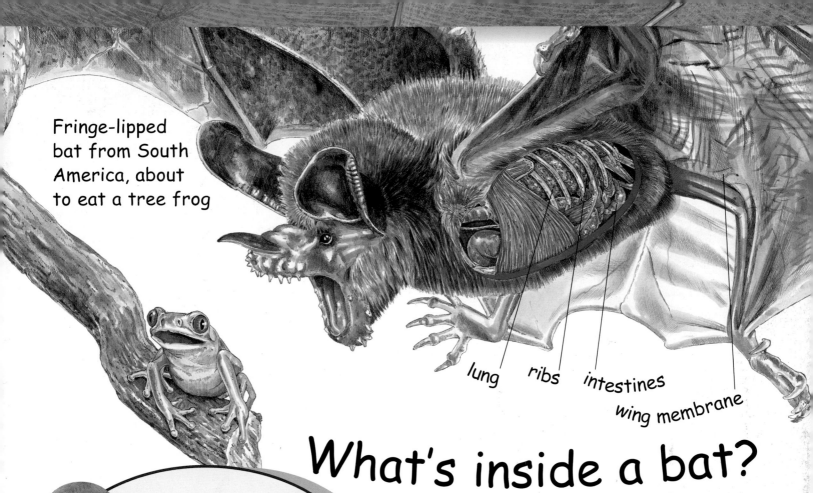

Fringe-lipped bat from South America, about to eat a tree frog

lung ribs intestines

wing membrane

What's inside a bat?

Bats and human beings are mammals. Inside their bodies they have the same kinds of bones, although bat bones are much smaller than ours. Bats' leg bones trail out behind narrow hips and help support the wings, along with the arm bones and long, slender fingers.

What are bats' teeth like?

Insect-eaters have small, pointed teeth for crunching up their prey, while bats that hunt larger animals have long canines for stabbing. Most fruit bats have large, flat molars for crushing. Vampire bats have very sharp teeth for slicing through skin.

Different kinds of bats have different teeth.

Can bats walk?

Some insect-eating bats can scurry along if they have to, but many bats cannot walk and actually avoid landing on the ground. If they do end up there they find it very difficult to take off again. There is one group of bats that lands on the ground all the time – vampire bats. They feed on the blood of large animals and usually creep quietly up to their prey.

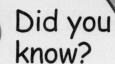
Unlike most bats, vampire bats can use their wings like another pair of legs. After landing silently near their sleeping prey, they slowly walk on all fours towards it (see (1) and (2) below).

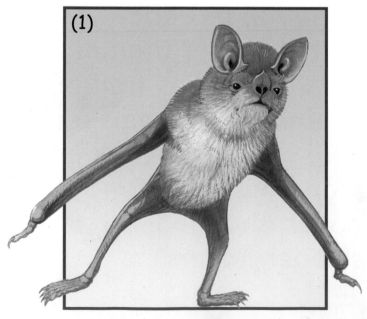

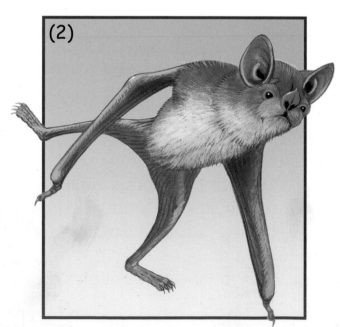

A bat's movements while 'walking'

Common pipistrelle bat crawling over a rock

If they need to, vampire bats can also hop and leap over the ground (see (3) and (4) below).

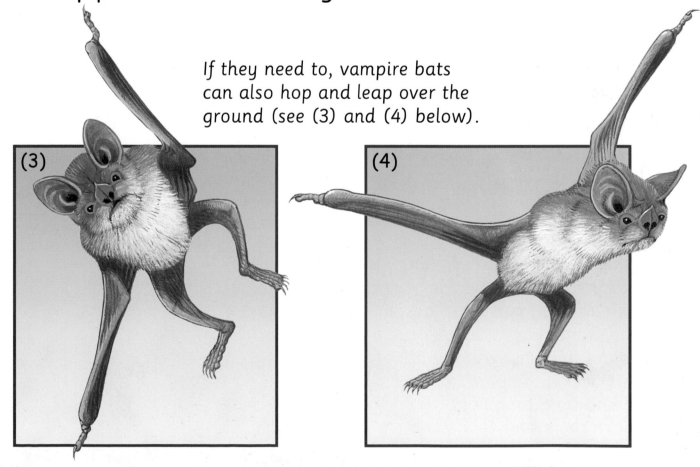

(3)

(4)

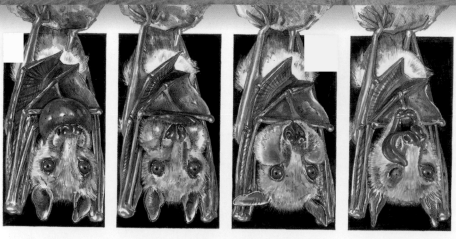

Wahlberg's epauletted bat eating a fig

Most fruit bats roost in trees by day and seek out their food at night. Wahlberg's epauletted bat (left), from Africa, feeds on figs. It takes them to a safe perch and hangs upside down to eat.

What do bats eat?

Bats eat a wide variety of food. Most of the smaller species feed on insects, such as moths, but some hunt animals almost as large as themselves. Vampire bats live entirely on a diet of blood and there are even bats that feed on fish. Flying foxes and their relatives eat the fruit that can be found in forests. Other bats feed on nectar from flowers, licking it out with especially long tongues.

Southern long-nosed bat

North America's southern long-nosed bat (right) feeds on nectar from the flowers of cacti and other desert plants. Sometimes it lands on the plant itself but usually it hovers over it, dipping its nose and long tongue in to reach the sweet, sticky food.

Fringe-lipped bat, eating a frog

Fringe-lipped bats (above) only hunt frogs that are harmless. All frogs have their own call and this bat ignores those of poisonous species. The fringe-lipped bat is one of several bats that hunts large prey.

The Australian ghost bat kills and eats frogs, lizards, mice, birds and even other bats. It hunts among trees and undergrowth, often flying low over the ground. Small creatures may be eaten on the wing (without landing) but larger prey is usually taken back to the roost in a cave or hollow tree.

How do bats hunt?

Bats hunt at night, in the dark. Although their eyes do work, most rely on other senses to find their prey. Insect-eating bats catch moths in mid-air by using echolocation. They emit high-pitched squeaks and clicks, and then wait to hear if any echoes return to them. If the sound wave from a squeak or click bumps into a moth some of the sound will bounce back. Most insect-eating bats' ears are specially tuned to pick up these echoes from prey.

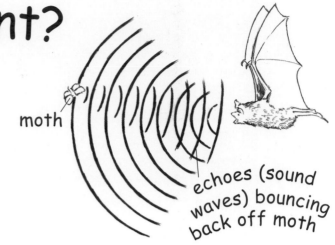

moth

echoes (sound waves) bouncing back off moth

Using echolocation to find prey

By measuring the time from click to echo a bat's brain is able to work out how far away a moth is (above). If the echoes from repeated clicks start returning faster, the bat knows that it is getting closer to its prey. If the echoes take longer and longer to return, it knows the moth is moving away.

Most insect-eating bats have very sensitive hearing. Their huge ears act as funnels, amplifying sound.

Many echolocating bats make sounds through their nostrils. Some, such as this giant spear-nosed bat (right), have specially shaped noses thought to help change or focus the sounds.

Giant spear-nosed bat

False vampire bat catching a mouse

It is not just insect-eaters that use echolocation. Bats that hunt larger animals use it too. This false vampire bat (above) uses echolocation to home in on a mouse, which it then takes away to its roost to eat.

Did you know?

Bats can 'see' using echolocation. As well as helping them hunt, they use it to avoid obstacles when flying, such as other bats in the pitch black of caves.

Why do bats hang upside down?

Bats hang upside down because of the way that their legs are positioned. A bat's legs stick out from the back of its body, partly because they help to hold its wings open in flight. Because of this, many bats find it almost impossible to stand up and take off from a flat surface. To get into the air, they take off by dropping from a height.

The claws on bats' toes are shaped like hooks (see opposite) and can only grip firmly if they have a weight hanging beneath them. Most fruit bats use their hooked toes to hang from the branches of trees. Because they are lighter, smaller bats can cling to tiny overhangs and ledges on the roofs of caves.

X-Ray Vision

Hold the page opposite up to the light and see what's inside a flying fox.

See what's inside

Spectacled flying fox

Bats have a hook-shaped claw on the thumb bone of their wings (left). They use this claw to help them move around while hanging upside down (above).

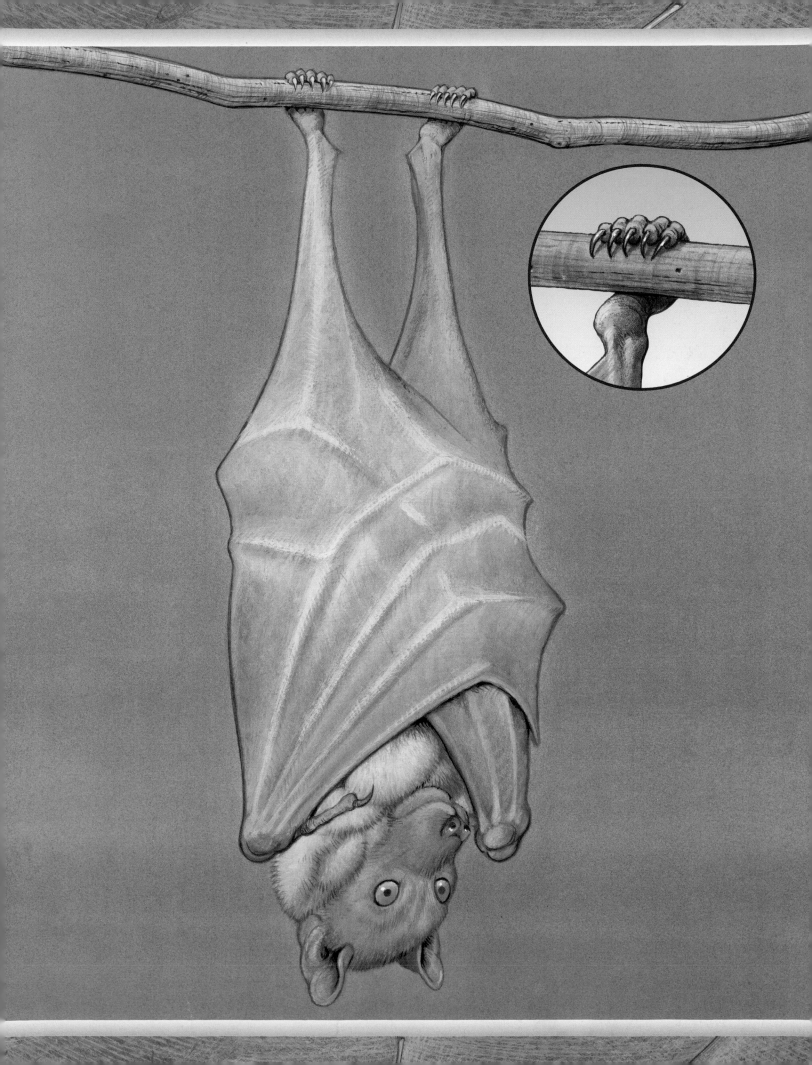

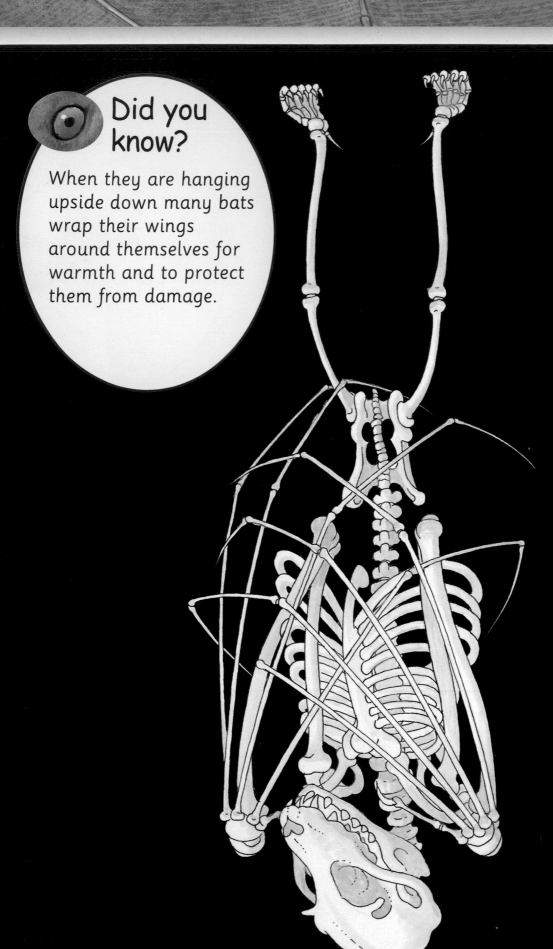

Did you know?

When they are hanging upside down many bats wrap their wings around themselves for warmth and to protect them from damage.

Skeleton of a flying fox with its wings wrapped around itself

Do bats hibernate?

Some bats hibernate in the winter to save energy. When hibernating, bats have a much lower heart rate than when they are active. Their body temperatures drop, sometimes as low as 0°C – the freezing point of water. When hibernating, bats can survive for months on their fat reserves alone. If they did not hibernate, most bats in cold climates would starve to death at this time of year, since food is often hard to find.

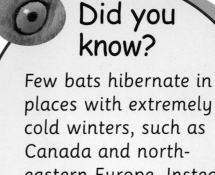

Did you know?

Few bats hibernate in places with extremely cold winters, such as Canada and north-eastern Europe. Instead, most fly south in autumn to warmer places and hibernate there.

Greater horseshoe bats roosting

Greater horseshoe bats hibernate huddled together for warmth. These greater horseshoes (left) are just roosting – when they hibernate, they wrap their wings around their bodies.

The mouth of a common vampire bat

Are vampire bats real?

Vampire bats are real, but they are not something to worry about. Vampire bats feed on the blood of other animals. All three species of vampire bat live in South and Central America. Two species are rare and mainly target roosting birds. The third species, the common vampire bat, gets its meals from mammals, including humans.

How do vampire bats feed?

To feed, vampire bats cut out a small piece of flesh with their razor-sharp teeth. They then lap up the blood as it flows from the wound. Special substances in their saliva prevent the blood clotting before they finish their meal.

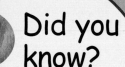

Did you know?

Vampire bats must drink half their own bodyweight in blood every day to survive. Bats too ill to hunt are fed by other colony members, which regurgitate blood for them when they return.

Vampire bats drink blood from their prey.

Vampire bats search for their prey by sight, smell and echolocation. Once a bat has found a victim, it uses its heat-sensitive nose to locate an area rich in blood vessels before it bites.

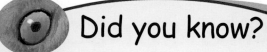

Did you know?

In 1988, the bones of giant vampire bats were found in a cave in Venezuela. Scientists think that these giant vampires are now extinct, although a recent find in Argentina included bones that were just 300 years old.

Vampire bat with outstretched wings

Can bats spread disease?

Most bats are harmless but some can spread disease. The worst disease that bats may carry is rabies, which is deadly to humans if left untreated. In Britain few people are ever bitten by bats, so the risk of catching rabies from one is very small.

Did you know?

In 1991, vampire bats caused a rabies epidemic in a town in Brazil. Driven from their natural homes by logging, several colonies of the bats descended on the town one night.

Leaf-nosed bat

However, the chance of catching rabies from a vampire bat bite is quite high. Every year, dozens of people in South America catch rabies from vampire bats. The numbers would be much higher if humans were the bats' main prey, but most vampire bats feed on wild animals or livestock such as cattle.

Most bats have teeth sharp enough to break the skin if they bite. Usually though, the only people who get bitten by bats are those who work with them, such as scientists and conservationists. These people have regular injections to prevent them developing rabies.

Like vampire bats, mosquitoes feed on blood. In tropical countries, many mosquitoes carry the disease malaria and pass it from bats to humans.

Did you know?

Mosquitoes are far more dangerous than bats. Every year, over a million people around the world die from malaria transmitted by mosquitoes. Many more become ill but recover from the disease.

Mosquito feeding on a person

A model bat used to frighten people at Halloween

Bats are creatures of the night that roost in churches and abandoned tombs. They have long been linked with Halloween.

Why are bats scary?

People who are afraid of bats usually do not understand them. They think that bats might be dangerous animals that could attack them or they just think they look frightening. Some people are scared of bats because of stories they have heard. For instance, it has been said that bats sometimes fly into women's hair and get tangled up. This is totally untrue, but many people still believe such stories.

Hammer-headed fruit bats (right), found in Asia, Northern Australasia and Africa are perhaps one of the most strange-looking types of bat. They are completely harmless to humans.

26

Scene from the 1922 vampire film *Nosferatu*

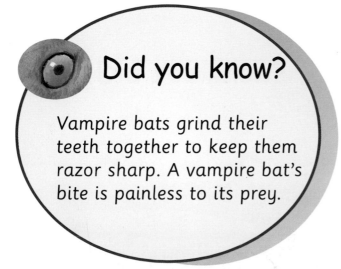

Did you know?

Vampire bats grind their teeth together to keep them razor sharp. A vampire bat's bite is painless to its prey.

Centuries ago, bats were often linked with witchcraft and the devil. More recently they have become tied up with tales of vampires. The idea of human vampires turning into bats was invented by the Irish writer Bram Stoker in his novel *Dracula*, published in 1897. The first film based on Stoker's book was called *Nosferatu* (above). Released in 1922, it featured a very bat-like vampire.

Bats around the world

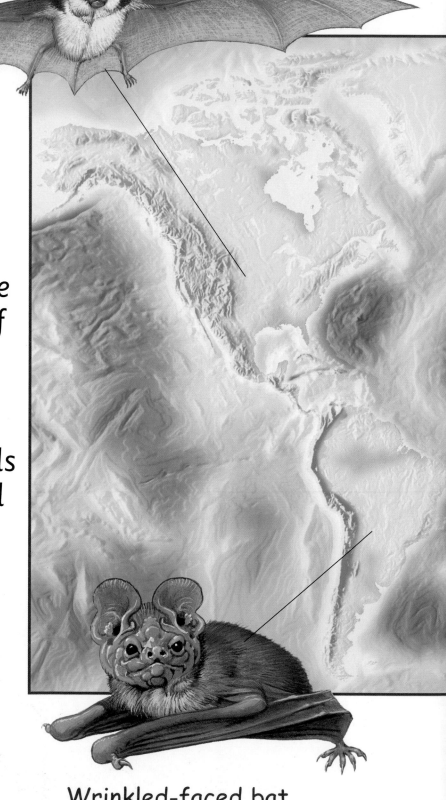

Spotted bat

Bats live all over the world and can be found on every continent except Antarctica. Bats make up about a quarter of all mammal species and they are usually the first mammals to appear on new islands after they are created by volcanoes. On many islands they are still the only mammals today.

Wrinkled-faced bat

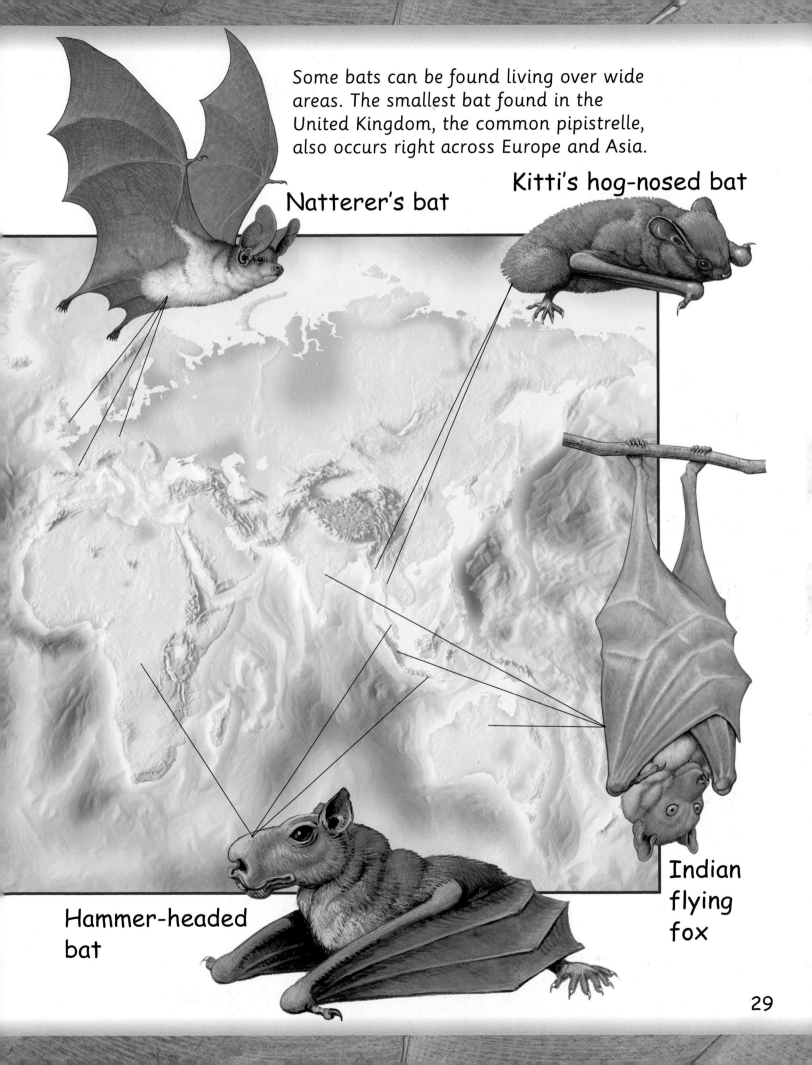

Some bats can be found living over wide areas. The smallest bat found in the United Kingdom, the common pipistrelle, also occurs right across Europe and Asia.

Natterer's bat

Kitti's hog-nosed bat

Hammer-headed bat

Indian flying fox

29

Bat facts

Bats' wings heal incredibly fast. Holes repair themselves in a matter of days. Even their finger bones heal very quickly if broken.

The fishing bat of South America catches fish from rivers at night. Using echolocation, it detects the ripples that fish produce when they are at the surface. It then flies over the water's surface, dragging the hooked claws of its feet through the water to grab its prey.

More than three-quarters of all bats are insect-eaters.

The largest flying foxes have wingspans of up to 2 metres.

Some insect-eating bats have membranes of skin between their legs and tail which they use to scoop flying moths from the air.

The smallest bat, Kitti's hog-nosed bat, has a wingspan of just 8 cm.

Honduran white bats make waterproof shelters by gnawing along the mid-ribs of large leaves. The sides of the leaves flop down, forming tent-like structures under which the bats roost, safe from tropical downpours.

Most bats roost and give birth in colonies. The largest known bat colony forms each summer in a huge cave near San Antonio, Texas. As many as 20 million Mexican free-tailed bats gather there to give birth.

Some bats use their thumb claws to manipulate food. Male flying foxes also use them for fighting. Fruit bats can use their feet and hooked thumbs to climb 'hand over hand' beneath branches.

The Rodrigues flying fox lives on the tiny island of Rodrigues in the Indian Ocean and is found nowhere else in the world.

South America's fringe-lipped bat specialises in hunting frogs. It finds its food by listening for the calls of male frogs, which croak through the night to attract females.

Some fruit bats raid banana plantations and other places where tropical fruit is grown, making them unpopular with farmers. However, without bats, many of these fruits would not grow in the first place – nectar-eating bats are often the main pollinators of tropical fruit trees.

Glossary

amplify To turn up or increase a sound.

canines The four pointed teeth mammals have in-between their incisors and molars.

colony A group of animals living together.

conservationist A person who works to protect wildlife or wild places.

continent A very large landmass. There are seven continents: North America, South America, Europe, Africa, Asia, Australia and Antarctica.

endangered Animals that are few in number and may be close to extinction.

epidemic A widespread outbreak of a disease.

hibernate To sleep through the winter.

mammal An animal that feeds on its mother's milk when it is a baby.

molars Back teeth used for grinding or chewing.

nectar A sweet, sticky liquid produced by flowers to attract animals.

pollination Taking pollen from a male flower to a female flower so that seeds and fruit will form.

prey Any animal that is hunted by other animals for food.

regurgitate To bring up food from the stomach.

rodent A small mammal with gnawing teeth such as a mouse, rat or squirrel.

roost Settle to rest or sleep.

species A group of living things that look alike, behave in the same way and can interbreed.

Index